Andy Warhol: Portraits of the 70s

Random House in association with the Whitney Museum of American Art, New York

Andy Warhol: Portraits of the 70s

Essay by Robert Rosenblum

Edited by David Whitney

This book was published in conjunction with an
exhibition held at the Whitney Museum of American
Art, November 20, 1979 – January 27, 1980

Copyright © 1979 by the Whitney Museum of
American Art. Introduction Copyright © 1979 by
Robert Rosenblum.
All rights reserved under International and
Pan-American Copyright Conventions. Published
in the United States by Random House, Inc., New
York and simultaneously in Canada by Random
House of Canada Limited, Toronto.

Library of Congress Cataloging in Publication Data

Warhol, Andy, 1928-
Andy Warhol, portraits of the seventies.
A catalog published to coincide with a major
exhibition opening at the Whitney Museum,
Nov. 20, 1979.
1. Warhol, Andy, 1928- Exhibitions.
2. Biography – 20th century – Portraits – Exhibitions.
I. Rosenblum, Robert. II. Whitney Museum of
American Art, New York. III. Title.
NB2237.5.W37A4   1979   759.13   79-4852
ISBN 0-394-50656-1
ISBN 0-394-73738-5 pbk.
ISBN 0-394-50655-3 lim. ed.

Manufactured in the United States of America
98765432
First Edition

Foreword

Andy Warhol once asked me to write a foreword to a catalogue of his work being published in a foreign language. I submitted my work to Fred Hughes and asked timidly, "How does Andy like it?" He responded, "Who cares? We won't be able to read it." Well, Andy, you will be able to read this one because it's in pure, simple English and it is my revenge for all those yeahs and gee whizzes and gollies that have endeared you to me over the past decade. Andy Warhol — this quiet, omnipresent being who commands our respect and asks for nothing but receives all. Unlike any other, Andy has a sense of the times, and he has sustained his magic for a long duration. Turning to portraits as a phase in his work, he has become the limner of our times. His portraits, as Robert Rosenblum so brilliantly describes, are the symbols of a culture which simultaneously dismisses symbols and yet craves them as marks of acceptability in Andy's world.

The Whitney Museum of American Art presented a retrospective exhibition of the work of Andy Warhol in 1971. We are pleased to continue our commitment to this outstanding American artist with this exhibition and catalogue of a particular phase of his work. We are indebted to David Whitney, who has organized the exhibition and assisted in the design of the book and in the exhibition installation at the Museum. Thanks also to the lenders who modestly disguised their vanity. Robert Rosenblum responded immediately to our request to write about Andy and vigorously went about his task, producing an essay about the artist unlike any written before.

It is difficult to know what will survive our times. However, my money is on Andy Warhol. He disgusts some, elates others, but is ignored by very few. His portraits are the image of a time when the tinsel and glitter is important and the superficial is paramount. The lip gloss of today is the sheen of tomorrow and Andy has recorded every brilliant highlight. One of the gratifications of presenting the work of an outstanding artist is reaffirmation of confidence in what he accomplishes. I have never wavered from the mark with Monsieur Warhola. As I said in the infamous foreign-language preface, when the last lifeboat is launched I want old Blondie at the oars.

Tom Armstrong, Director
Whitney Museum of American Art

Andy Warhol: Portraits of the 70s

Andy Warhol: Court Painter to the 70s   Robert Rosenblum

If anybody had been asked in the 1950s to check the pulse of contemporary portraiture, the diagnosis would have been gloomy. "Moribund" might have said it discreetly; "Dead" would have been more like it. Were any humanoid presence to emerge from that distant, mythic world conjured up by Rothko, Newman, and Pollock, it could only have been the Holy Shroud, Adam, or Thor; and even if one of de Kooning's women were to congeal into an identifiable being, she would probably turn out to be Lilith or the Venus of Willendorf. The prospects of any mortal, not to mention contemporary, man or woman surfacing in that lofty pictorial environment seemed slim indeed.

But art and history are full of surprises, and few were more startling than the way the younger generation of the 1960s wrenched the here-and-now (which are now the then-and-there) facts of American life back into art. The doors and windows of the ivory-tower studios were suddenly opened wide, and the pure air inside was instantly polluted (or some would say rejuvenated) by the onslaught of the ugly but irrefutably vital world outside. Of the many things that demanded immediate attention, from city streets, highways, and supermarkets to billboards, newspaper print, and television sets, the pantheon of 1960s celebrities was high on the list. If everybody in the civilized and not-so-civilized world instantly recognized Elvis Presley or Marlon Brando, why should their images be censored out of the history of serious art? If a pall was cast on this whole planet in the summer of 1962 when news of Marilyn Monroe's suicide instantly circled the globe, why shouldn't a painter commemorate her for posterity? If, in the following year, Jacqueline Kennedy helped the nation and the world bear their collective grief by maintaining a public decorum worthy of a Roman widow, why shouldn't there have been a living artist who could record for future generations this modern Agrippina? Luckily, there was.

Andy Warhol, in fact, succeeded virtually single-handed in the early 1960s in resurrecting from near extinction that endangered species of grand-style portraiture of people important, glamorous, or notorious enough — whether statesmen, actresses, or wealthy patrons of the arts — to deserve to leave their human traces in the history of painting. To be sure, this tradition, which grew ever more feeble in the twentieth century, occasionally showed a spark of life in the hands of a few ambitious painters, above all in England. Here one thinks of Graham Sutherland's portraits of the 1950s and 1960s of the likes of Lord Clark, Sir Winston Churchill, Helena Rubinstein, Dr. Konrad Adenauer, or the Baron Elie de Rothschild, where the tradition of Titian, Velázquez, and Reynolds seems not quite to have given up its ghosts and where, for a moment, the sharp facts of universally known physiognomies seem to blend with a pictorial environment of old-masterish resonance and aristocracy. And a decade or two earlier, and again in England, one thinks of the neglected late portraits of Walter Sickert, who, in the 1920s and 1930s, often used for his depictions of eminent contemporaries the most informal news photographs, which provided an underlying image of reportorial truth for, say, a glimpse of King George V and Queen Mary passing by in a royal automobile or of King Edward VIII greeting troops. Indeed, as Richard Morphet has already proposed, there are prophecies of Warhol in Sickert's strange amalgams of London press photos and the lofty traditions of state portraiture.[1]

More often than not, however, paintings of public figures in the last decades belong, especially in the United States, to the domain of Portraits, Inc., and its ilk. When confronted with the prospects of eternity in depicting a great man of state, most official painters rattle around in a graveyard of

Graham Sutherland
Helena Rubinstein in Red Brocade Balenciaga Gown, 1957
Oil on canvas, 61″ x 36″
Collection: The Helena Rubinstein Foundation, New York

traditions. A pretty funny case in point is Wayne Ingram's portrait-apotheosis of Lyndon Baines Johnson in the LBJ Library, in Austin, Texas, where the thirty-sixth President of the United States first faces us real as life, and then ascends, via a shower of de Kooning-plus-LeRoy Neiman brushstrokes, to a secular baroque heaven where his watchful spirit still floats on high.

It was Warhol's masterstroke to realize (as Sickert and even Bacon had tentatively suggested in eccentric ways) that the best method of electrifying the old-master portrait tradition with sufficient energy to absorb the real, living world was, now that we see it in retrospect, painfully obvious. The most commonplace source of visual information about our famous contemporaries is, after all, the photographic image, whether it comes from the pages of the *Daily News* or *Vogue.* No less than the medieval spectator who accepted as fact the handmade images of Christian characters who enacted their dramas within the holy precincts of church walls, we today have all learned to accept as absolute truth these machine-made photographic images of our modern heroes and heroines. When Warhol took a photographic silkscreen of Marilyn Monroe's head, set it on gold paint, and let it float on high in a timeless, spaceless heaven (as Busby Berkeley had done in 1943 for a similarly decapitated assembly of movie stars in the finale of *The Gang's All Here*), he was creating, in effect, a secular saint for the 1960s that might well command as much earthly awe and veneration as, say, a Byzantine Madonna hovering for eternity on a gold mosaic ground. And when he reproduced the same incorporeal divinity not as a single unit, holy in its uniqueness, but as a nonstop series, rolling off an invisible press in endless multiples, he offered a kind of religious broadsheet for popular consumption, suitable to the staggering, machine-made quantities of our time, where the tawdry imperfections of

Walter Sickert
King George V and Queen Mary, 1935
Oil on canvas, 25″ x 29¾″
Collection: Sir Colin and Lady Anderson

Wayne Ingram
Portrait of President Lyndon B. Johnson, 1968
Oil on canvas, 48″ x 36″
Collection: The Lyndon Baines Johnson Library
and Museum, Austin, Texas

Andy Warhol
Gold Marilyn Monroe, 1962
Acrylic and silkscreen enamel on canvas, 8 3¾" x 57"
Collection: The Museum of Modern Art, New York
Gift of Philip Johnson

smudged printer's ink or off-register coloring have exactly the ring of commonplace truth we recognize from the newspapers and cheap magazines that disseminated her fame.

By accepting the photograph directly into the domain of pictorial art, not as an external memory prop for the painter's handmade re-creation of reality but as the actual base for the image on canvas, Warhol was able to grasp instantly a whole new visual and moral network of modern life that tells us not only about the way we can switch back and forth from artificial color to artificial black-and-white on our TV sets but also about the way we could switch just as quickly from a movie commercial to footage of the Vietnam war. For Warhol, the journalistic medium of photography, already a counterfeit experience of the world out there, is doubly counterfeit in its translation to the realm of art. He takes us into an aestheticized Plato's cave, where the 3-D facts outside, whether concerning the lives of a superstar or an anonymous suicide, are shadowy fictions of equal import. In terms of portraiture, this second-degree reality dazzlingly reinforces the inaccessible human presence of those remote deities — a Liz Taylor or a Happy Rockefeller — whom only a select few have actually seen at eye level in three corporeal dimensions; and in terms of our more general awareness of what is really happening on the other side of our movie and TV screens, it frighteningly reflects exactly the way in which, for the television generation, which has now become our future population, the eyewitness fact of Jack Ruby's on-the-spot shooting of Lee Harvey Oswald in a Dallas police station was almost to be confused with the fictional murders that followed and preceded this real-life, but scarcely believable, event on the same channel.

That Warhol could paint simultaneously Warren Beatty and electric chairs, Troy Donahue and race

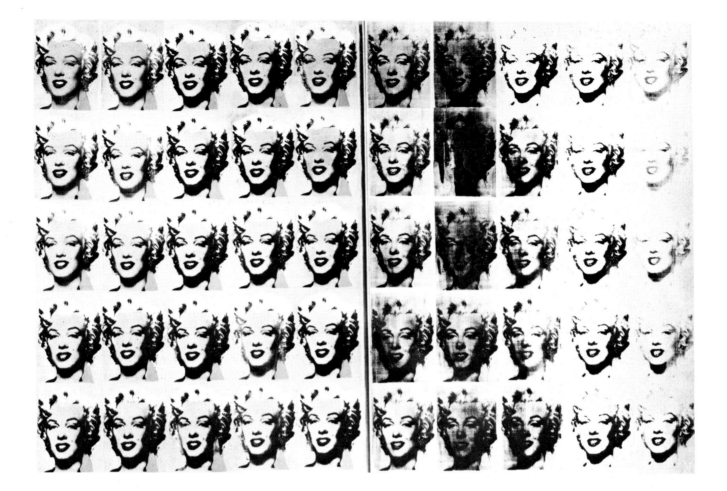

Andy Warhol
Marilyn Monroe Diptych, 1962
Acrylic and silkscreen enamel on canvas
2 panels, each 82″ x 57″
From the Collection of Mr. and Mrs. Burton Tremaine,
Meriden, Connecticut

riots, Marilyn Monroe and fatal car crashes, may seem the peculiar product of a perversely cool and passive personality until we realize that this numb, voyeuristic view of contemporary life, in which the grave and the trivial, the fashionable and the horrifying, blandly coexist as passing spectacles, is a deadly accurate mirror of a commonplace experience in modern art and life. It found its first full statement, in fact, a century earlier in the work of Manet. Like Warhol, Manet wears the disguise of an aesthete-reporter whose camera-eye range extended from the haut monde of famous people (from Mallarmé and George Moore to Clemenceau and Chabrier), of proto-Fauchon luxury edibles (from salmon and oysters to brioche and asparagus), and of pampered dogs (from poodles to terriers), all the way to contemporary events which would earlier have been interpreted as harrowing tragedies (a bullfighter killed in the ring, a barbaric execution of an Austrian emperor, a hair-raising maritime escape of a political prisoner from a penal colony, an unidentified man who has just shot himself on a bed). The familiar complaint that Manet painted the harshest facts of death with the same elegant detachment, cold-blooded palette, and unfocused composition that he used for still lifes, picnics, pet animals, and society portraits is one that could be leveled at Warhol. But in both cases, it perhaps is not blame but gratitude that we owe these artists for compelling us to see just how false our conventional moral pieties are when judged against the truth of our usual shoulder-shrugging responses to what often ought to be the shattering news of the day. And in both cases these reportorial observations about the facts of modern life are lent further distance by being seen literally through a pictorial skin that insistently calls attention to itself. The subtle chill of Manet's and Warhol's view of current events through the aesthete's tinted glasses often cuts more deeply than the louder screams of Expressionist psychology.

For Warhol's seeming moral anesthesia, his poker-faced rejection of the conventional hierarchies of the tragic and the silly, become still more detached and ironic through his manipulation of the look of commercial photography as a new vocabulary to be explored as an aesthetic language in itself. The blurrings of printer's ink, the misalignment of contours, the flat graininess of shadows, the brusque and arbitrary change from one colored filter to another, the new plastic spectrums of chemical hues both deadly and gorgeous — such products of the mechanized world of photographic printing and retouching are isolated by Warhol and provide him with a fresh range of visual experiences that usurp the earlier artifices of picture-making. They become, in fact, the stuff from which new cosmetic layers are made, ugly-beautiful paint surfaces that turn the truth of the silkscreened photographs on the canvas into a distant shade of an ever more intangible reality.

The contradictory fusion of the commonplace facts of photography and the artful fictions of a painter's retouchings was one that, in Warhol's work, became a particularly suitable formula for the recording of those wealthy and glamorous people whose faces seem perpetually illuminated by the afterimage of a flashbulb, and whose physical reality might be doubted by the millions who recognize them. In the 1970s, Warhol's production of such society portraits accelerated to a point where he and his paintings constantly intersected the world of paparazzi and of high-fashion photography. If many of the celebrity portraits of the 1960s, whether of Jackie or Marilyn, smacked of the *New York Post* or *Screen Romances* and almost made us feel that our fingers might be stained with cheap newsprint if we touched them, those of the 1970s belong to the glossy domain of *Vogue* and Richard Avedon. The Beautiful People have replaced the dreams and nightmares of Middle

America; the world of the Concorde, that of the U.S. highway accident. From those first days of Bonwit Teller window displays and starry-eyed, adolescent pin-up fantasies, Warhol's upward mobility was supersonic. Instead of getting the super-stars' photos from movie magazines or the Sunday color supplement, he himself quickly invaded their society on equal terms, and could be begged by prospective sitters to turn his own Polaroid camera on their fabled faces in both public and private moods. He had become a celebrity among celebrities, and an ideal court painter to this 1970s international aristocracy that mixed, in wildly varying proportions, wealth, high fashion, and brains.

With Warhol's gallery of contemporary faces, the decade of 1970s high society is instantly captured. In this glittering realm, light and shadow are bleached out by the high wattage of spotlights; colors seem selected from the science-fiction rainbow invented by the likes of Baskin-Robbins; and brushstrokes offer an extravagant, upper-income virtuosity which appears to be quoting, for conspicuous consumption, a bravura tradition that extends from Hals through de Kooning. By comparison, the look of Warhol's 1960s paintings was often of lower-income austerity and dreariness, of Brillo boxes and Campbell's soup cans, of the faces of criminals, innocent victims, or remote superstars who could barely sparkle through the smeared newsprint. On more than one level, Warhol has wrapped up two decades for our social time capsule.

But however time-bound these portraits of the 1970s may be, they also belong to a venerable international tradition that had its heyday in the

Giovanni Boldini
Portrait of Mme. Charles Max, 1896
Oil on canvas, 89″ x 40″
Collection: Paris, Musée du XIXème Siècle — Orsay
Don de Mme. Charles Max en 1904

late nineteenth century. In the familiar way that new art alters our perception of old art, Warhol's society portraits may have given a fresh lease on life to the achievement of those moneyed, high-fashion portraitists who, at the turn of the last century, were feted as honored guests in the drawing rooms and villas of the fabled patrons whom they also painted? This lustrous roster can count as members the Italian Giovanni Boldini, the Spaniard Joaquín Sorolla, the Swede Anders Zorn, the American John Singer Sargent, the Frenchmen Jules Clairin and Jacques-Emile Blanche, and hordes of others who aspired to be accepted as equals in the company of Sarah Bernhardt and Ellen Terry, Marcel Proust and Henry James, Isabella Stewart Gardner and Mrs. Potter Palmer. The Warholian connections here are not only social but aesthetic. In a typical Boldini portrait, that of Mme. Charles Max of 1896, the truths of physiognomy, of mannered gesture, and designer clothing are first seized, but then submerged under a pictorial veil of artifices, which here include fencing-lesson brushstrokes that evoke the most supple human animation but are then contradicted by grisaille tonalities that immobilize the sitter in an environment of chilly aristocracy.

That Warhol himself is hardly unaware of this tradition is evident in, for instance, his choices for the "Raid the Icebox" exhibition held (1969–70) at the Rhode Island School of Design, in Providence, where he was allowed to select a show from the storage vaults and came up with, among other things, some late-nineteenth-century American examples of this elegant, brushy portrait tradition by William Merritt Chase and Frank Benson, as well as sterner royal prototypes from earlier decades, such as Joseph Paelinck's state portraits of King William and Queen Hortense, the Napoleonic rulers of the Dutch Netherlands. (It should be no surprise

Raid the Icebox 1 With Andy Warhol, 1969–1970
Museum of Art
Rhode Island School of Design, Providence

Allan Ramsay (Copy After)
King George III, 1761
Oil on canvas, 90" x 57"

Allan Ramsay (Copy After)
Queen Charlotte, 1761
Oil on canvas, 90" x 57"

either that Warhol's 1978 auction-purchases included first-class replicas of Allan Ramsay's full-length coronation portraits of King George III and Queen Charlotte, which, like many official royal portraits of the eighteenth and nineteenth centuries, were turned out by highly skilled assistants in the artist's studio as multiples for wider image distribution. As usual, Warhol has shrewd intuitions about his own art-historical pedigree.)

If it is instantly clear that Warhol has revived the visual crackle, glitter, and chic of older traditions of society portraiture, it may be less obvious that despite his legendary indifference to human facts, he has also captured an incredible range of psychological insights among his sitters. From the utter vacuity of the camera-oriented smile of the wife of an international banker to the startling disclosures of moods fit for private diary, these painting-snapshots add up to a Human Comedy for our time, in which pictorial surface and psychological probing are combined in differing proportions and in which the very existence of not one but two or more variations on the same photographic fact add to the complex shuffle of artistic fictions and emotional truths.

Take the pair of Liza Minnelli portraits. What we may first see is how a familiar face is flattened to extinction by the blinding glare of a flashbulb or by the cosmetic mask of lip gloss, hair lacquer, mascara. Almost like Manet in *Olympia*, Warhol has here retouched reality to push his pictorial facts to a two-dimensional extreme. Middle values vanish (the nose and shoulders are swiftly ironed out to the flatness of paint and canvas), and we are left with so shrill and abrupt a juxtaposition of light and dark that Courbet's quip about *Olympia's* resemblance to the Queen of Spades might be repeated here. But as in *Olympia,* this insistent material façade of opaque, unshadowed paint cannot annihilate a psychological presence. From behind this brash silhouette, a pair of all too human, almost tearful eyes returns our gaze.

Or take the portraits of Ivan and Marilynn Karp. Even if we don't know that Ivan, the art dealer, thinks, moves, and talks faster and clearer than most of us mortals, Warhol has told us all by fixing a momentarily steady gaze, in synch with the cool puff of a cigar, amid a nervous flutter of brushwork that first dissolves the hand and then leaves centrifugal traces of wriggling, linear energy at the edges of hair, shoulder, lapel. As for his wife, Marilynn, a counterpersonality is instantly indicated by Warhol's revival, so frequent in these portraits, of Picasso's use of a profile on a frontal view to evoke an external-internal dialogue with the more concealed recesses of psychology. Here, the furtive glance of the pink profile, underscored by a stroke of blue eyeshadow, is given even greater emotional resonance by the murky glimpse of the far side of the face, which anxiously meets our gaze from the deepest shadows.

The range of human revelation, both of public and private personality, is no less dazzling in these portraits than their seductive surfaces. (For comparison, one might check the inert products of an imitator like Rodney Buice, who uses the Warhol formula for everyone from Arnold Schwarzenegger to Prince Charles.) Here are Leo Castelli, at his dapper and urbane best; Alexander Iolas, in an intimate glimmer of frightening vulnerability worthy of the portrait of Dorian Gray; Brooke Hayward, at once ravishingly worldly and devastatingly innocent;

Andy Warhol
Mao, 1973
Acrylic and silkscreen enamel on canvas
176½'' x 136½''
Collection: The Metropolitan Museum of Art
Gift of Sandra Brant, 1977

Carolina Herrera, a queen tigress among tiger-women; Henry Geldzahler, his cigar and elusive gaze forever poised for public view; Sofu Teshigahara, in a cool flash of yen-to-dollar business acumen; David Hockney, with that beguiling shock of blond hair above a lovably callow face; John Richardson, in a sinister, black-leather mood; Marella Agnelli, a living embodiment of patrician elegance and hauteur; and Norman Fisher, as a bone-chilling phantom, a white-on-black negative image all too grimly appropriate to a posthumous portrait of a snuffed-out life.

Even when Warhol leaves, from time to time, the jet-set world of art, business, fashion, the results are equally incisive. It is something of a miracle that a contemporary Western artist could seize, as Warhol has, the Olympian Big Brother image of Mao Tse-tung. In a quartet of canvases huge enough to catch one's eye at the Workers' Stadium in Peking, Warhol has located the chairman in some otherworldly blue heaven, a secular deity of staggering dimensions who calmly and omnipotently watches over us earthlings. Not since the days of rendering Napoleon as God or Jupiter has an artist come to successful grips with the frighteningly serene and remote authority of the leader of a modern totalitarian state. One need only look at Warhol's cornily matter-of-fact portraits of the all too earthbound and fallible Gerald Ford and Jimmy Carter to realize how much has been said.

At the opposite end of Mao's daunting image of inscrutable power, the posthumous portraits of Julia Warhola, the artist's mother, cast an alien spell. That she has gained access at all to this International Portrait Gallery may not be so surprising when one remembers that another famous artist-dandy, Whistler, could paint, almost as pendants, portraits of both his mother and Thomas Carlyle, as if the sitters' human realities were secondary to the decorative realities asserted by the artist's titles, "Arrangement in Grey and Black, Nos. 1 and 2." But if Warhol's aestheticism is often close to that of the nineteenth century, implying that all is sheer surface and that art levels out the distinction between great men and flower arrangement, here, with Julia Warhola, the posture cracks. For beneath these virtuoso variations, there presides in both clear focus and ghostly fade-outs a photographic image of a bespectacled old lady, the artist's mother, a haunting memory at once close and distant. In the midst of this racy and ephemeral company of *Women's Wear Daily* and *Interview,* her glamourless countenance is all the more heart-tugging, an enduring and poignant remembrance of family-things past. She reminds us of the last thing we expected to think about in Warhol's fashionable Hall of 1970s Fame: that art and life, that personal and public history may overlap but, in the end, are very different things.

Notes:

1. Richard Morphet, "The Modernity of Late Sickert," *Studio International,* vol. 190 (July–August 1975), pp. 35-38.

2. Warhol's relation to this tradition of upper-class portraiture has already been pointed out in David Bourdon's excellent and informative article, "Andy Warhol and the Society Icon," *Art in America,* vol. 63 (January–February 1975), pp. 42-45.

Andy Warhol
Julia Warhola, 1974
Acrylic and silkscreen enamel on canvas
40" x 40"

Plates

Giovanni Agnelli, 1972   25

Marella Agnelli, 1972

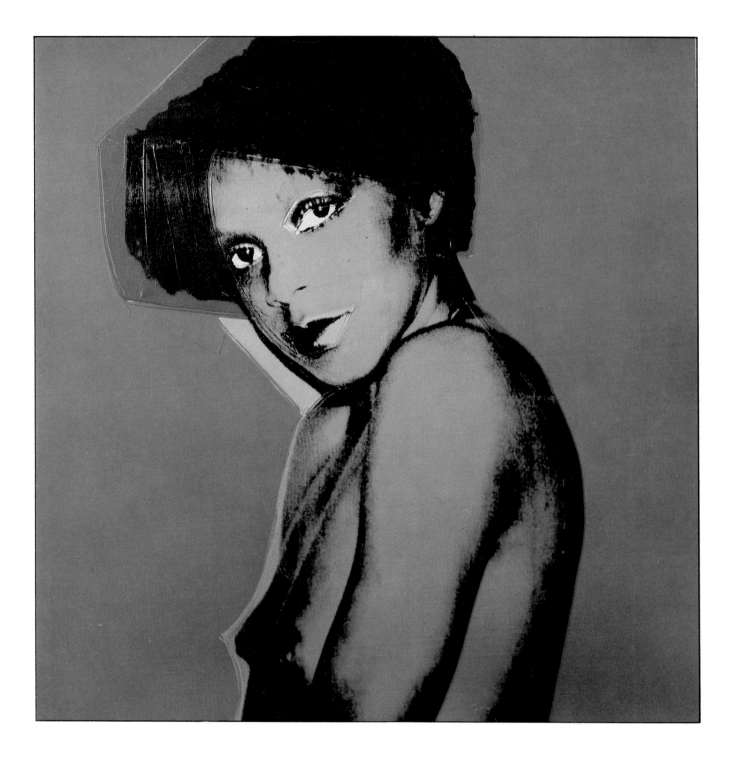

Corice Arman, 1977   29

Marion Block, 1975   31

Irving Blum, 1970   33

Truman Capote, 1979   35

Cristina Carimati, 1978   37

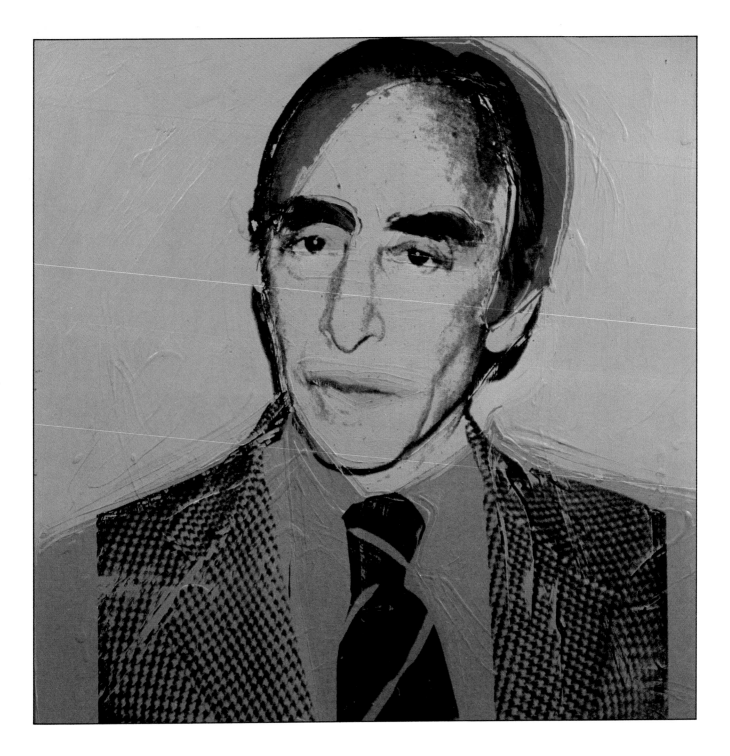

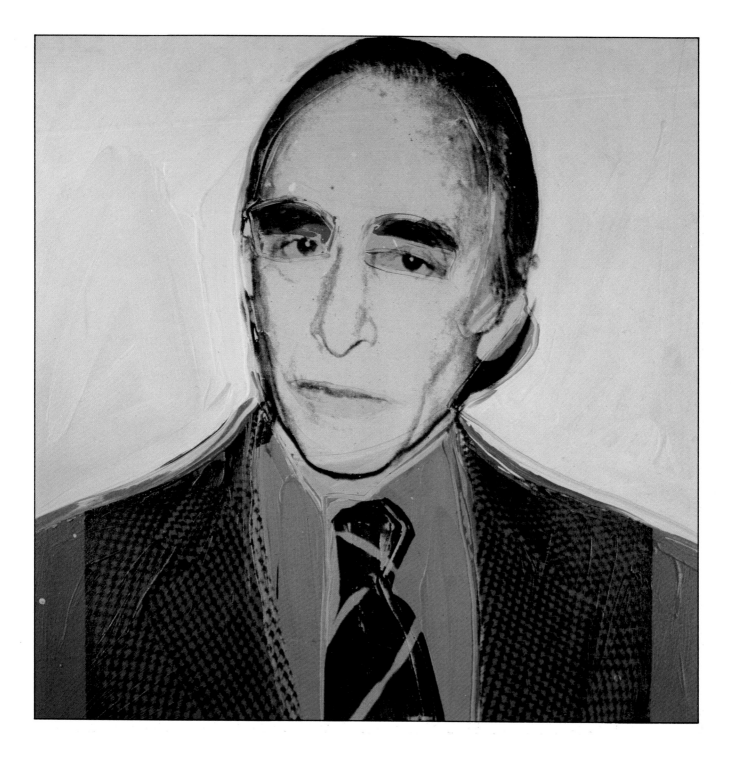

Leo Castelli, 1975   39

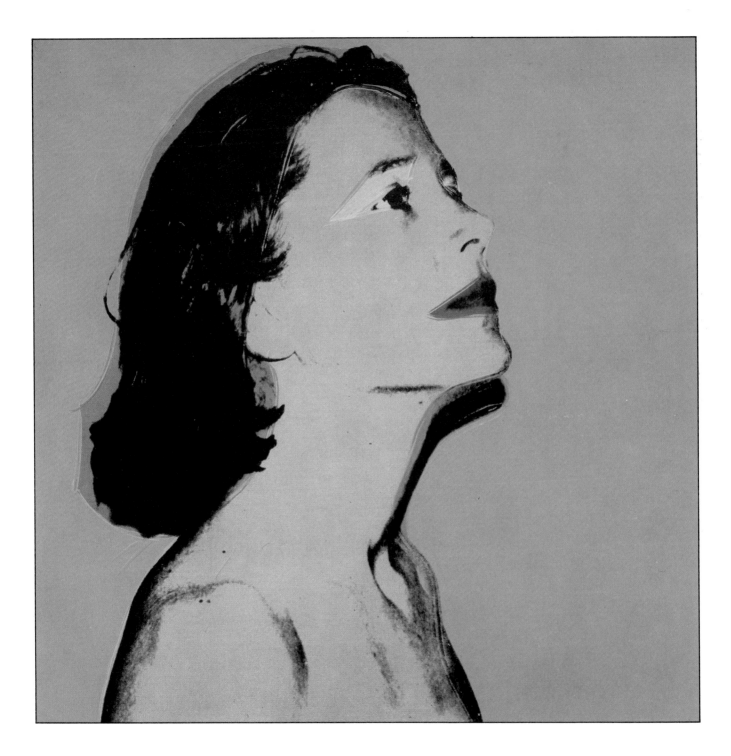

Carol Coleman, 1976   41

Norman Fisher, 1978   43

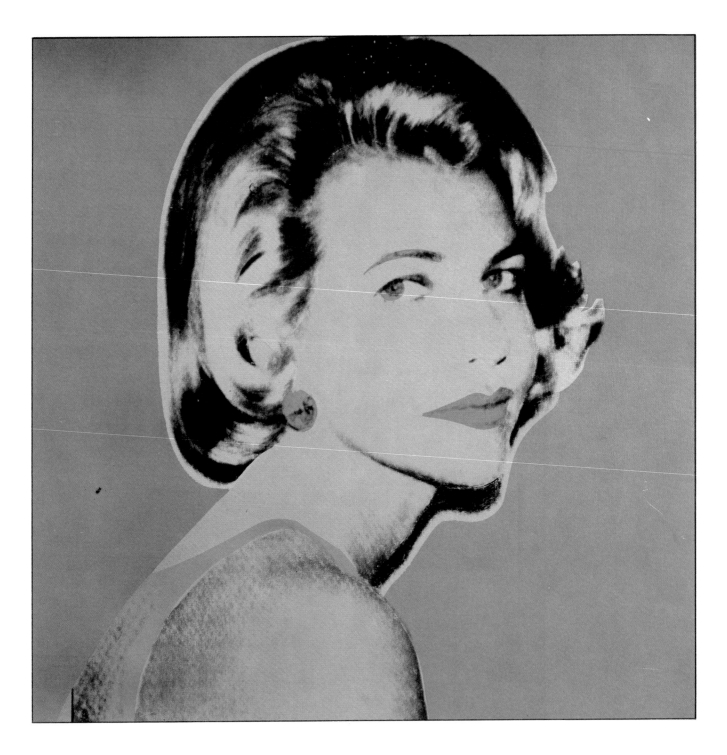

44

Kay Fortson, 1977   45

Tina Freeman, 1975   47

Diane von Furstenberg, 1974   49

Henry Geldzahler, 1979   51

Halston, 1974   53

Brooke Hayward, 1973   55

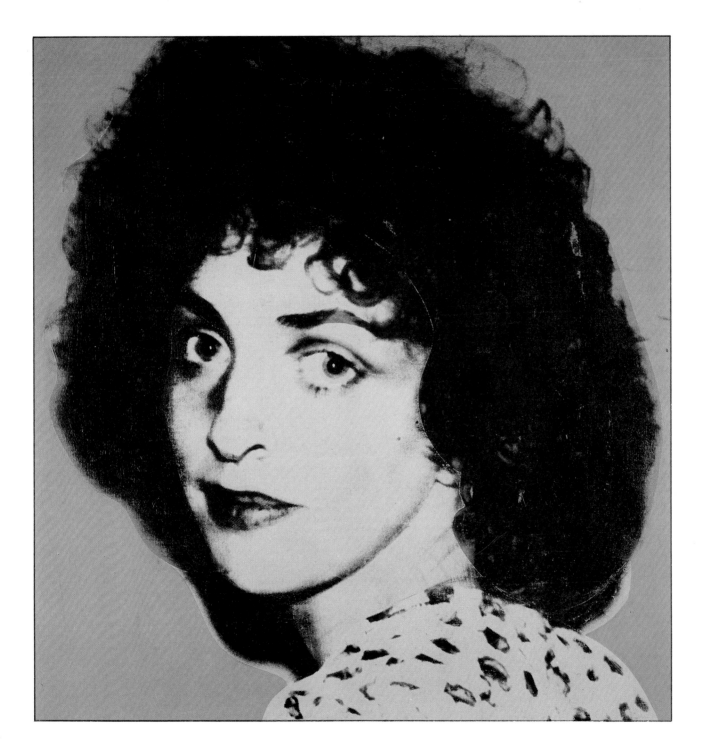

Barbara Heizer, 1978   57

Michael Heizer, 1978   59

Carolina Herrera, 1979   61

David Hockney, 1974 63

Jane Holzer, 1975   65

Dennis Hopper, 1970　67

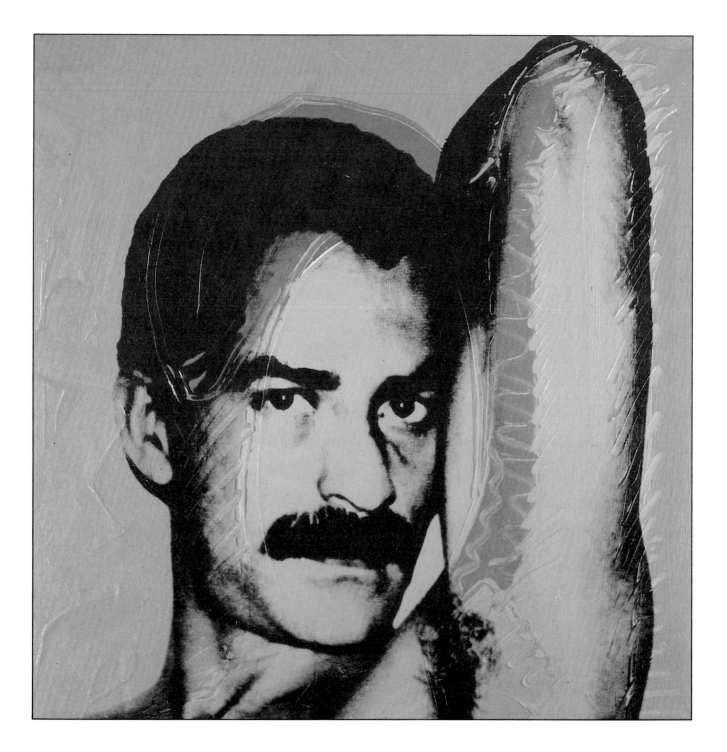

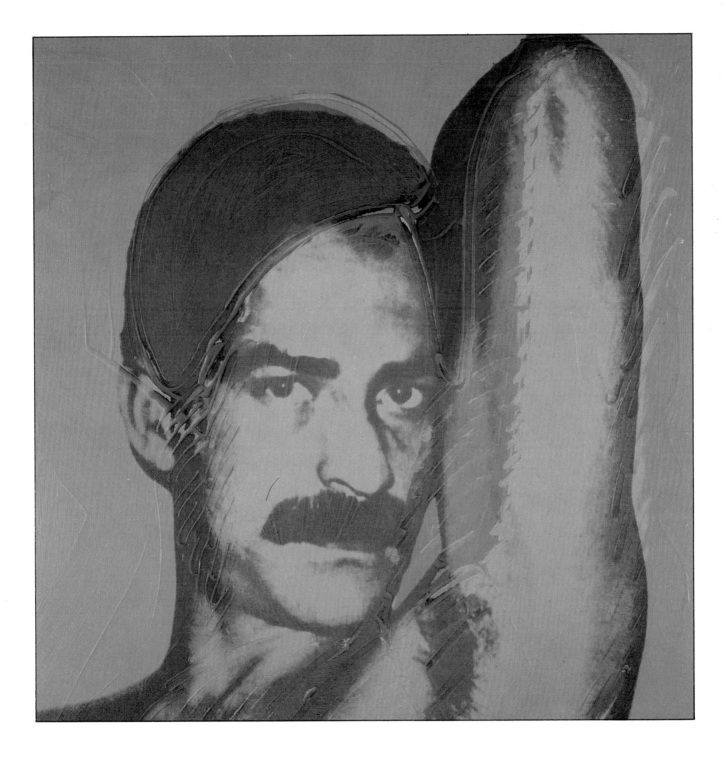

Victor Hugo, 1978   69

Alexandre Iolas, 1971   71

Caroline Ireland, 1979   73

Charles Ireland, 1979   75

Mick Jagger, 1976   77

Paul Jenkins, 1979   79

Katie Jones, 1973   81

Ivan Karp, 1974   83

84

Marilynn Karp, 1975   85

Evelyn Kuhn, 1977   87

Jane Lang, 1976   89

Frances Lewis, 1973   91

Sydney Lewis, 1973   93

Dorothy Lichtenstein, 1974   95

Roy Lichtenstein, 1976   97

Daryl Lillie, 1979   99

Joe Macdonald, 1975   101

Erich Marx, 1978   103

Golda Meir, 1975   105

Liza Minnelli, 1978

Lynda Palevsky, 1974   109

Kimiko Powers, 1971-72   111

John Richardson, 1974   113

Helene Rochas, 1975   115

Yves St. Laurent, 1974   117

Gale Smith, 1978   121

Ileana Sonnabend, 1973   123

Sofu Teshigahara, 1976   125

Janet Villella, 1979　127

Doda Voridis, 1977   129

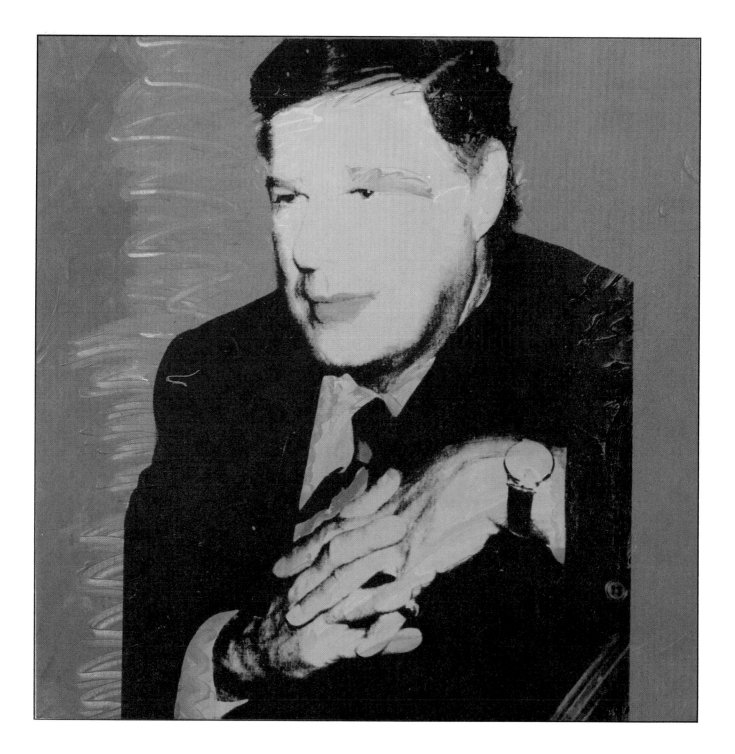

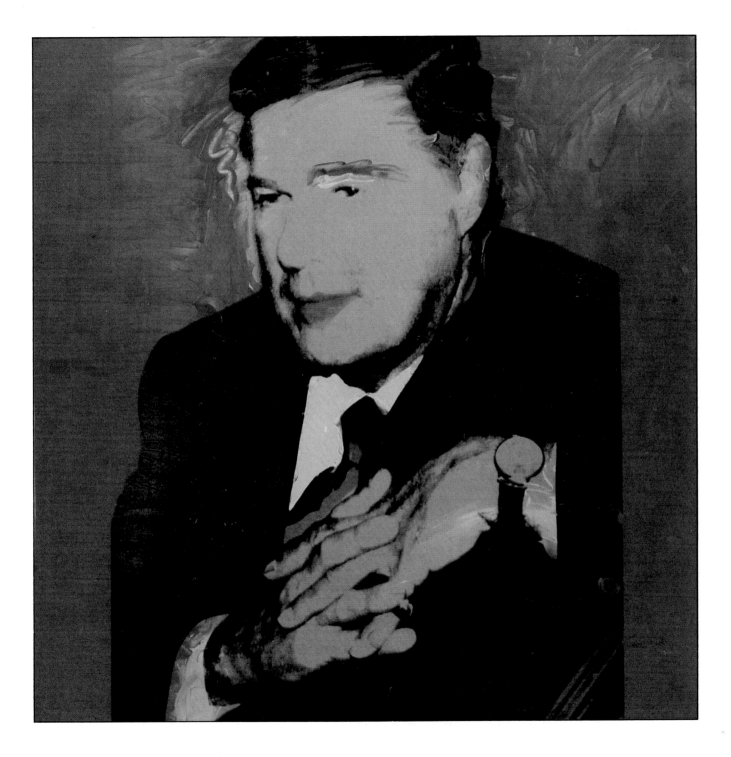

Frederick Weisman, 1974   131

Marcia Weisman, 1975   133

Jamie Wyeth, 1976　135

List of Illustrations

All portraits are acrylic and silkscreen enamel on canvas, 40''x 40''. There are two panels of each subject.

Giovanni Agnelli, 1972
Collection: Giovanni Agnelli

Marella Agnelli, 1972
Private collection

Corice Arman, 1977
Collection: Corice Arman

Marion Block, 1975
Private collection

Irving Blum, 1970
Collection: Irving Blum

Truman Capote, 1979
Private collection

Cristina Carimati, 1978
Carimati Collection

Leo Castelli, 1975
Collection: Leo Castelli Gallery (one panel)
Private collection (one panel)

Carol Coleman, 1976
Private collection

Norman Fisher, 1978
Collection: Keith Sonnier (one panel)
Private collection (one panel)

Kay Fortson, 1977
Collection: Mr. and Mrs. Ben J. Fortson, Fort Worth, Texas

Tina Freeman, 1975
Collection: Tina Freeman

Diane von Furstenberg, 1974
Collection: Diane von Furstenberg

Henry Geldzahler, 1979
Collection: Paul Jenkins (one panel)
Private collection (one panel)

Halston, 1974
Collection: Halston

Brooke Hayward, 1973
Collection: Brooke Hayward

Barbara Heizer, 1978
Collection: Michael Heizer (one panel)
Private collection (one panel)

Michael Heizer, 1978
Collection: Barbara Heizer (one panel)
Private collection (one panel)

Carolina Herrera, 1979
Private collection

David Hockney, 1974
Private collection, England

Jane Holzer, 1975
Collection: Jane Holzer

Dennis Hopper, 1970
Private collection

Victor Hugo, 1978
Private collection

Alexandre Iolas, 1971
Private collection

Caroline Ireland, 1979
Collection: Charles W. Ireland

Charles Ireland, 1979
Private collection

Mick Jagger, 1976
Private collection

Paul Jenkins, 1979
Collection: Paul Jenkins

Katie Jones, 1973
Private collection

Ivan Karp, 1974
Private collection

Marilynn Karp, 1975
Private collection

Evelyn Kuhn, 1977
Private collection

Jane Lang, 1976
Collection: Mr. and Mrs. Richard E. Lang, Medina, Washington (one panel)
Seattle Art Museum, Gift of Mr. Richard E. Lang, 76.47 (one panel)

Frances Lewis, 1973
Collection: Sydney and Frances Lewis

Sydney Lewis, 1973
Collection: Sydney and Frances Lewis

Dorothy Lichtenstein, 1974
Collection: Dorothy and Roy Lichtenstein

Roy Lichtenstein, 1976
Collection: Dorothy and Roy Lichtenstein (one panel)
Private collection (one panel)

Daryl Lillie, 1979
Collection: Daryl L. and John M. Lillie (one panel); private collection (one panel)

Joe Macdonald, 1975
Collection: Joseph Macdonald (one panel)
Private collection (one panel)

Erich Marx, 1978
Private collection

Golda Meir, 1975
Sydney and Frances Lewis Collection

Liza Minnelli, 1978
Collection: Halston

Lynda Palevsky, 1974
Collection of Lynda and Max Palevsky

Kimiko Powers, 1971-72
Collection: Mrs. Constance Powers (one panel)
Mr. and Mrs. S. R. Weintraub (one panel)

John Richardson, 1974
Private collection

Helene Rochas, 1975
Private collection

Yves St. Laurent, 1974
Collection: Yves St. Laurent

Sao Schlumberger, 1976
Collection: Mme. Sao Schlumberger

Gale Smith, 1978
Collection: Gale and David Smith

Ileana Sonnabend, 1973
Collection: Mr. and Mrs. Michael Sonnabend

Sofu Teshigahara, 1976
Private collection

Janet Villella, 1979
Collection: Janet Villella

Doda Voridis, 1977
Private collection

Frederick Weisman, 1974
Collection of Mid-Atlantic Toyota Distributors, Inc., Glen Burnie, Maryland

Marcia Weisman, 1975
Frederick Weisman Family Collection

Jamie Wyeth, 1976
Courtesy Coe Kerr Gallery